LOOKING BACK

INDIA UNDER THE
MUGHAL
EMPIRE
1526-1858

LOOKING BACK

INDIA UNDER THE
MUGHAL
EMPIRE
1526-1858

ANITA GANERI

RSVP
RAINTREE
STECK-VAUGHN
PUBLISHERS
A Steck-Vaughn Company

Austin, Texas

Editors: Nicola Barber, Pam Wells
Designer: Neil Sayer
Picture research: Victoria Brooker
Maps: Nick Hawken
Production: Jenny Mulvanny

Consultant: Dr. Avril Powell, School of Oriental and African
               Studies, University of London

Library of Congress Cataloging-in-Publication Data

Ganeri, Anita, 1961-
      India under the Mughal Empire, 1526-1858 / Anita Ganeri.
           p.   cm. — (Looking back)
      Includes index.
      Summary: Looks back at the reigns of the six greatest
Mughal emperors, from Babur to Aurangzeb, and at the decline
of the empire during the rise of British rule in India.
      ISBN 0–8172–5432-3
      1. Mughal Empire — History — Juvenile literature.
[1. Mughal Empire.]   I. Title.   II. Series.
DS461.G26   1999
954 .02'5 — dc 21   98-6042
                                                               CIP   AC

Printed in Spain
Bound in the United States
1 2 3 4 5 6 7 8 9 0 LB 02 01 00 99 98

Acknowledgments

Cover (Main image) Trip/H Rogers (Background image) Victoria and Albert Museum/Bridgeman Art
Library **Title page** Chester Beatty Library and Gallery of Oriental Art, Dublin/Bridgeman Art Library
page 7 Ancient Art and Architecture **page 8** Pankaj Shah **page 9** T Gervis/Robert Harding Picture
Library **page 10** Musee Conde, Chantilly, France/Giraudon/Bridgeman Art Library **page 11** Trip/H
Rogers **page 12** Private Collection/Bridgeman Art Library **page 13** JHC Wilson/Robert Harding
Picture Library **page 14** Robert Harding Picture Library **page 17** (top) Ancient Art and Architecture
(bottom) Bridgeman Art Library **page 18** British Library, London/Bridgeman Art Library **page 19**
National Museum of India, New Delhi/Bridgeman Art Library **page 20** Werner Forman Archive
page 21 Ancient Art and Architecture **page 23** Chris Oxlade **page 24** British Museum/Bridgeman Art
Library **page 26** Pankaj Shah **page 27** Victoria and Albert Museum/Bridgeman Art Library
page 29 Ancient Art and Architecture **page 30** National Museum of India, New Delhi/Bridgeman Art
Library **page 31** Chris Oxlade **page 32** Victoria and Albert Museum/Bridgeman Art Library **page 34**
British Library/Bridgeman Art Library **page 35** Private Collection/Bridgeman Art Library **page 36**
Robert Harding Picture Library **page 37** (top left) Ancient Art and Architecture (bottom right) e.t.
archive **page 38** Chris Oxlade **page 39** Chester Beatty Library and Gallery of Oriental Art,
Dublin/Bridgeman Art Library **page 43** Ancient Art and Architecture **page 44** e.t. archive **page 46**
(top) Victoria and Albert Museum/Bridgeman Art Library (bottom) British Library/Bridgeman Art
Library **page 47** Private Collection/Bridgeman Art Library/Bonhams UK **page 49** Victoria and Albert
Museum/Bridgeman Art Library **page 50** Victoria and Albert Museum/Bridgeman Art Library
page 51 National Museum of India, New Delhi/Bridgeman Art Library **page 52** Pankaj Shah **page 53**
Chris Oxlade **page 55** Ancient Art and Architecture **page 56** Werner Forman Archive **page 57** British
Library/Bridgeman Art Library **page 58** e.t. archive **page 59** British Library/Bridgeman Art Library

CONTENTS

INTRODUCTION

At the height of its power in the 16th and 17th centuries, the Mughal (Mogul) Empire covered almost the whole of India (apart from its southernmost tip) and ruled the lives of between 100 and 150 million people. Its leaders were Muslim princes whose ancestors came from Afghanistan and Uzbekistan to the northwest. They established one of the largest and most splendid empires ever seen, creating brilliant military and administrative systems in order to expand and rule their territories. The Mughal court was famous for its dazzling luxury, its exquisite buildings and paintings, its literature and beautiful gardens. At the center stood the imposing figure of the emperor, around whom the workings of the empire revolved. This book looks back at the reigns of the six greatest Mughal emperors, from Babur to Aurangzeb. It ends with the decline of the empire and the rise of British rule in India.

NORTHWEST INVADERS

The Mughals were not the first people to invade India from the northwest. Over the centuries many other groups vied for power in this region. In about 1500 B.C., groups of Indo-Europeans from Central Asia arrived in northwest India, spreading through the valley of the Indus River and down into the Ganges Valley. From the 6th to the 4th centuries B.C., the province of Gandhara in northwest India was ruled by Persians. Centuries later, in the 5th century A.D., the mighty Gupta Empire covered most of northern

A CLOSER LOOK

At the time of the Mughals, India covered a much larger area than it does today. It included present-day Pakistan, Bangladesh, and parts of Afghanistan, Nepal, and Myanmar (Burma), all of which are now independent countries. The Mughals did not use the name India. They called the country Hindustan, which means "Land of the Hindus [Indians]" in Persian.

India until it was weakened by invasions of the Hun people from Central Asia.

The Muslim invasion of India began in earnest in A.D. 1001 with a series of raids by the Turk, Mahmud of Ghazni, who ruled in Afghanistan (see page 13). By 1236 the Delhi Sultanate, founded by Mahmud's successors, had become the greatest power in northern India (see page 15). The Delhi Sultanate was a Muslim kingdom, named after the title of its Muslim ruler, the Sultan, with power centered in Delhi. Three hundred years later, control of the Sultanate had passed to the Mughals.

HOW DO WE KNOW?

Our knowledge of the Mughal Empire comes from a variety of sources. Many of the emperors kept detailed memoirs, which they dictated to trusted scribes or secretaries. These gave details of their daily routines, likes and dislikes, important events at court, battles, and so on. They were not always accurate — it was sometimes diplomatic for a scribe to embellish, or add to, the emperor's words and describe him in more glowing terms than he deserved! The manuscripts were illustrated with exquisite paintings, showing scenes from court life and portraits of courtiers. These paintings provide modern historians with much valuable information. Accounts were also written by European visitors to the Mughal court, all of whom were astonished by what they saw. Back in Europe, their gripping tales of the fabulous wealth and power of the Great Mughals quickly became very popular.

An illustration from the Akbar-nama, *the memoirs of Akbar, the third great Mughal emperor. It shows a battle scene. Painters sometimes accompanied the emperor into battle to record events as they happened.*

RELIGIONS IN INDIA

Hindus worship many gods and goddesses. They visit a mandir (temple) to view the deity that is represented by a sacred image, such as this one. This caused conflict with the Muslims who do not allow such figures to be shown.

For centuries, India has been a melting pot for many of the world's major religions — Hinduism, Islam, Buddhism, Sikhism, and Jainism. There are also communities of Parsis (Zoroastrians), Jews, and Christians. At the time of the Mughals, Hinduism was, as it is now, the largest religion in India, with Hindus making up over three-quarters of the population. The Mughals were Muslims, followers of Islam. In India the two religions frequently clashed. But the two also worked together to create, for example, new schools of architecture and painting, formed from a mixture of Hindu and Muslim styles. The amount of tolerance that existed between Hindus and Muslims largely depended on the attitude of each individual emperor. Their points of view ranged from Akbar's respect for other religions to the intolerance of Aurangzeb, a strict Muslim.

HINDUISM

Hinduism is one of the world's oldest religions, with roots reaching back over 4,000 years to the time of the Indus valley civilization in northwest India. This civilization collapsed in about 2000 B.C. but its religious beliefs combined with those of later Indo-European invaders to form the basis of Hinduism.

Hindus believe in a supreme being, called Brahman, whose characteristics and powers are represented by three main gods – Brahma the creator of the universe, Vishnu the protector, and Shiva the destroyer – and by hundreds of other different gods and goddesses.

Hindu society has traditionally been divided into four classes, or castes: Brahmins (priests), Kshatriyas (soldiers and nobles), Vaishyas (merchants), and Sudras (laborers). Outside the caste system were millions of people who did the dirtiest jobs, such as sweeping the streets.

The Jain temple in Ranakpur, Rajasthan, one of the largest and most important Jain temples in India. Built in 1439, this huge temple has 29 halls carved from marble. Inside are statues of the 24 prophets.

BUDDHISTS AND JAINS

In the 6th century B.C. two religions began in northern India — Buddhism and Jainism. The founder of Buddhism was a nobleman, Siddhartha Gautama, who left behind a life of luxury to seek the true meaning of life. After he had gained enlightenment, he traveled around India teaching his message, or *dharma*. In the 3rd century B.C., under Emperor Ashoka, Buddhism flourished and began to spread farther out to Sri Lanka, Thailand, and China. However, by the 12th century A.D., after the revival of Hinduism and arrival of Islam, Buddhism had almost disappeared from India.

The Jain religion was founded by a contemporary of the Buddha, called Mahavira. He was the 24th and last of the Jain prophets, known as *tirthankaras*. Jains share many beliefs with Buddhists, including that of *ahimsa*, or non-violence. This means showing respect for all living things, however small, and not harming or killing them. Jainism is still strong in western India, where it began, but it has not had much impact elsewhere.

ISLAM

The Mughals, and the earlier Sultans of Delhi, brought a new religion into India — Islam. Islam was founded by the Prophet Muhammad in Mecca, Arabia, in about A.D. 620. In a series of revelations, Muhammad received the message of Islam from God, that there is only one God, called Allah. These revelations were later written down as the *Koran*, the holy book of Islam. Within a few years of Muhammad's death in A.D. 632, most of Arabia had been converted to Islam. Within a century, Islam had reached as far west as Spain and North Africa, and as far east as Turkey, Persia, and the northwest frontiers of India.

In the mid-16th century, the Mughal Empire was one of three great Islamic empires in Asia. The mighty Ottoman Empire in Turkey was founded in

Two pages from a beautifully decorated copy of the Koran, *the holy book of the Muslims. It tells Muslims how to worship and how to live their lives. It is written in Arabic.*

the 13th century and was finally brought to an end in World War I (1914-18). Both the Mughals and Ottomans clashed frequently with the rulers of the third Muslim empire, the Safavids in Persia.

THE RISE OF THE SIKHS

The Sikh religion was founded in the Punjab, northwest India, in about A.D. 1500 by a holy man called Nanak. Nanak's parents were Hindus, but

Guru Nanak, the founder of the Sikh religion. Despite Mughal persecution, the influence of Sikhism grew steadily in northwest India.

they were accustomed to living and working side by side with the many Muslims who had settled in the region. Nanak's new religion stressed that everyone, Hindu or Muslim, was equal in God's eyes, regardless of outward differences. He himself is said to have dressed so that he could not be identified as either a Muslim or a Hindu, and to have made a point of visiting both Muslim and Hindu holy sites. Nanak was the first of ten Sikh gurus (teachers) who passed on Sikh beliefs for 200 years. At various times under Mughal rule, the Sikhs suffered persecution and oppression for their beliefs. In response the tenth Guru, Gobind Singh, founded the *Khalsa* (brotherhood) in 1699 (see page 41).

INDIA BEFORE THE MUGHALS

The Mughals were not the first Muslims to reach India. Merchants from Arabia had been trading with India for hundreds of years, exchanging horses, metals, and foodstuffs for precious Indian spices, silks, cottons, and gemstones. They took Indian techniques of rice cultivation and sugarcane production back to the Middle East. As knowledge increased about the seasonal monsoon winds in the first century B.C., Arab ships began to sail directly across the Arabian Sea between India and the Persian Gulf, rather than make the slower, riskier journey along the coast. The region of Malabar, on the west coast of India, became an important center for the spice trade. With the decline of Roman trade with India in the 4th century A.D., control of the main trading routes passed into Arab hands.

In A.D. 711, an Arab force conquered the western province of Sind, the region that lies around the delta of the Indus River. The Arabs introduced Islam to India. Being only a small community, they did not try to convert Hindus but gave them the special status of *zimmi*, or protected

A traditional Arab trading ship. Arab merchants had been trading with India for hundreds of years before the Mughal Empire.

peoples. They also respected the age-old Hindu caste system and left it in place. So the first contact between India and Islam was relatively peaceful.

MAHMUD OF GHAZNI

In A.D. 1001, Mahmud of Ghazni (ruled 999-1030) led the first of a series of bloody raids across the Afghan frontier into northwest India. A Turkish nobleman by birth, Mahmud ruled the kingdom of Ghazni in Afghanistan. Apart from spreading the word of Islam through *jihad* (holy war), his aim in India was to plunder the legendary wealth of the Hindu temples. By 1025 A.D., Mahmud and his men had sacked many of the prosperous temple cities of western India, stealing vast amounts of gold, jewelry, and money to refill his treasuries. He ordered sacred images of the Hindu deities, or gods, to be destroyed and left many of the temples in ruins. He also took over the rich crop-producing lands of the Punjab and added them to his empire.

In 1025, Mahmud attacked the great temple city of Somnath in Gujarat. The temple contained a

The great Hindu temple of Somnath, Gujarat, was said to have been built by the Moon god. So many pilgrims flocked to worship there that 300 barbers were employed to shave their heads (a sign of purity).

huge stone statue, which seemed to hang in midair without any means of support. Pilgrims flocked to worship in the temple, especially at times of eclipses of the Sun or Moon, and brought precious gifts as offerings. This is part of an Arab historian's account of the temple: "A thousand Brahmins worshiped the image continuously; and every night it was washed with fresh water from the Ganges, though the river was many miles away. A chain of gold, with bells fastened to it, was hung in a corner of the temple; it was shaken at the appointed hour to inform the Brahmins that the time for prayer had arrived. Five hundred singing and dancing girls and two hundred musicians were in the service of the temple, and all their needs were provided from the endowments and offerings. Three hundred barbers were employed to shave the heads and beards of the pilgrims."

Mahmud ordered the image to be smashed and the jewels, gold, and precious embroidered cloth that covered it to be taken back to Ghazni. Fifty thousand people were killed.

A CLOSER LOOK

The Qutb Minar in Delhi is a soaring victory tower, begun by Qutb-ud-Din Aibak in 1193. It was built to mark the Muslim defeat of the last Hindu kingdom in Delhi and the start of the Delhi Sultanate. The tower is 240 feet (73 m) high, with five stories made of red sandstone and marble. Qutb-ud-Din himself built only up to the first story; his sucessors completed the rest. At the foot of the tower, stands one of the first mosques ever built in India, the Might of Islam Mosque, also begun by Qutb-ud-Din. The original mosque was built on the foundations of a Hindu temple, using materials from the demolished temple.

The Qutb Minar, Delhi

MUHAMMAD OF GHUR

When Mahmud died in 1030, his place was taken by Muhammad of Ghur (ruled 1173-1206), leader of another group of Turks from Afghanistan. His campaign to conquer northwest India began in 1185 when he captured Lahore, now in Pakistan. Within 30 years, he had brought all of the region around the great plains of the Indus and the Ganges west of Varanasi under his command. In 1193, Muhammad seized control of Delhi and made it his headquarters. However, in 1206 Muhammad was assassinated, and his general, Qutb-ud-Din Aibak (ruled 1206-10), proclaimed himself the first Sultan of Delhi. A former slave, the dynasty he founded became known as the Slave Dynasty. It lasted until 1288, by which time the Delhi Sultanate was established as the largest and most powerful state in northern India.

THE DELHI SULTANATE

From its beginnings in the early 13th century to its eventual decline in the 16th century, the Delhi Sultanate was divided into different dynasties with more than 30 rulers. The Slave Dynasty of Qutb-ud-Din was followed by the Khaljis, also of Turkish stock. This period was marked by an increasing number of raids by the Mongols, members of nomadic tribes from the north. While trying to withstand these assaults, the Sultanate was also concerned with the task of imposing Muslim rule over the remaining Hindu kingdoms in India, such as the great Rajputs of Rajasthan in the west. Both

A CLOSER LOOK
Qutb-ud-Din Aibak was succeeded as Sultan by his son-in-law, Iltumish (ruled 1211-36). A firm and capable ruler, he strengthened and expanded the Sultanate's rule. When his eldest son died, he groomed his daughter, Raziya, to succeed him. Raziya reigned from 1236 to 1240 – the first woman to rule in the Islamic world. Though "wise, just, and generous" and "endowed with all the qualities befitting a king," she was resented by many of the Sultanate's ministers for being a woman and was murdered in 1240.

15

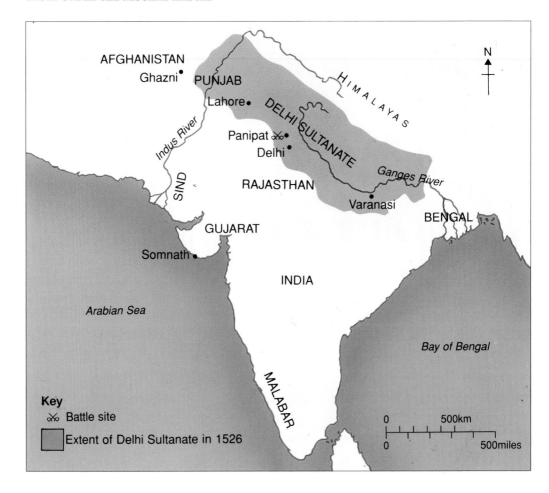

AFGHANISTAN
Ghazni
PUNJAB
Lahore
HIMALAYAS
Indus River
Panipat
DELHI SULTANATE
Delhi
SIND
RAJASTHAN
Ganges River
Varanasi
BENGAL
GUJARAT
Somnath
INDIA
Arabian Sea
Bay of Bengal
MALABAR

N

Key
Battle site
Extent of Delhi Sultanate in 1526

0   500km
0   500miles

The map shows the extent of the Delhi Sultanate at the time of its defeat by the Mughals in 1526. This event marked the beginning of the Mughal Empire in India.

campaigns took their toll on the Sultanate, and its resources were seriously stretched. From the end of the 14th century, its power began to decline. Territories were lost, and disputes broke out over who should rule. Some Hindu and Muslim states broke away from the Sultanate and declared their independence. However, a bigger threat was to come.

THE SACK OF DELHI

The worst of the Mongol raids happened in 1398 during the Tughluqid dynasty when the notorious and terrifying Mongol leader, a Turk called Timur (or Tamerlane), led his armies into India. He met little in the way of resistance. Timur arrived in India in September and by early December he had reached Delhi, stopping only to ransack the towns he passed through. Thousands of townspeople were captured as slaves. Outside Delhi an attack was launched by

The Mongol leader, Timur (1336-1405). His raid on Delhi was so ferocious, it was reported that nothing moved, not even a bird, for two months afterward.

the Sultanate on Timur's forces. On December 17, Timur beat back the Sultanate's army and entered the city in triumph. His officials were ordered to empty the treasuries, but the situation soon grew out of control. While Timur enjoyed a feast of celebration, the Mongol soldiers rampaged through Delhi, looting and pillaging. Thousands of people were taken prisoner. Thousands more were massacred. Ten days later, Timur left Delhi and set off for home, leaving utter devastation behind him.

THE BATTLE OF PANIPAT

Soon after Timur's terrible attack, the Tughluqid dynasty came to an end. It was replaced by the Sayyids who ruled a much weakened Sultanate for almost 40 years. In 1451 the Sayyids were ousted by Bahlul Lodi, an Afghan, who founded the Lodi dynasty. In 1526, at the Battle of Panipat, the last Sultan of Delhi was defeated and killed by Babur, the ruler of Kabul in Afghanistan, and a descendant of the mighty Timur. The Mughal Empire had begun.

A CLOSER LOOK

The great Muslim traveler and explorer, Ibn Battutah (1304-69), spent many years at the court of the Sultan of Delhi, Muhammad ibn Tughluq (ruled 1324-51). The Sultan received him well, appointed him a judge, and sent him as ambassador to China. Ibn Battutah left a detailed account of life at court, describing Delhi as the largest and most magnificent city in the Muslim world and the Sultan as "of all men the fondest of making gifts and shedding blood."

While in India, Timur took many skilled artists and stonemasons as prisoners. Then he had them work on his glittering capital at Samarkand. These craftworkers blended Indian and Persian styles together, for example in the design of this royal tomb.

FOUNDING AN EMPIRE

Babur's victory at the Battle of Panipat in 1526 marked the beginning of the Mughal Empire in India. Babur was the first of the six Great Mughals, the greatest rulers of the empire.

Emperor Babur sits on his throne, receiving visitors. Babur's reign lasted for only four years, from 1526-30.

BABUR

Able to trace his ancestry back both to Timur and to Genghis Khan, Babur had the perfect background for becoming a leader and general. Babur was born on February 14, 1483. His father was the ruler of the small province of Fergana, located in modern Uzbekistan. When Babur was 11 years old, his father died in a strange accident. One day, he was feeding his racing pigeons, which lived in a pigeon house on the outer wall of the palace, when the wall gave way, and he fell to his death. The young Babur succeeded to his father's throne and became one of a group of petty rulers in the region, all descended from Timur and related to each other. These small kingdoms were constantly jostling for power and fighting wars among themselves. Babur's fortunes rose and fell with those of the neighboring princes. He spent much of his time on the move, living in a camp, campaigning, or defending his territory.

CONQUEST OF INDIA

In 1496, when he was just 13 years old, Babur marched west, to lay siege to the famous city of Samarkand, Timur's glittering capital. He entered the city in triumph seven months later. But he held onto the city for only three months. A rebellion in Fergana called him home and ended with Babur losing his own kingdom to his younger brother. With a small band of followers, Babur spent many years living as a homeless wanderer, but he gradually won Fergana back. In 1504, having given up any hope of retaking Samarkand, Babur captured Kabul in Afghanistan.

In 1513, Babur turned his sights east toward India. Rumors reached him that all was not well with the Delhi Sultanate, and the Governor of the Punjab asked him for help. Babur invaded India

A CLOSER LOOK

Apart from being a brilliant soldier, Babur also loved books and poetry. He described his life and thoughts in his memoirs, the *Babur-nama*. Homesick for the hills of Kabul, his first impressions of India were not very good: "Hindustan is a country of few charms.... There are no good horses, no good dogs, no grapes, no muskmelons, or good fruits, no ice or cold water, no good bread or food in the bazaars, no hot baths, no colleges, no candles, torches, or candlesticks."

An illustration from Babur's memoirs, the Babur-nama, shows the emperor in one of the gardens that he loved. The Mughals created many beautiful, formal gardens in India to remind them of home.

The city of Jodhpur, in Rajasthan, is dominated by its magnificent fort. Jodhpur was founded in 1459 by Rao Jodha, a Rajput chieftain and is one of hundreds of forts in the region. The Rajputs were India's most famous Hindu warriors and the Mughals' toughest opponents.

several times before, on April 21, 1526, his troops came face-to-face with the Sultanate's forces at the Battle of Panipat near Delhi. Babur's army was heavily outnumbered. Sultan Ibrahim Lodi commanded some 100,000 men and 1,000 war elephants. Babur had 12,000 troops. But Babur also had light guns and muskets, new weapons from Turkey that helped to bring him victory. Ibrahim was killed and his army fled. Babur marched to Delhi, where he proclaimed himself emperor, then on to Agra, which became his new capital.

RAJPUT THREAT

The following year, in March 1527, Babur faced the mighty forces of the Rajputs of Rajasthan. The Rajputs were famous warriors from the state of Rajasthan in northwest India. For many years the Rajputs, who were Hindus, had fought to defend their independence from Muslim rule. They were becoming ever more powerful and were feared as the bravest warriors in India. Under the command of Rana Sangha of Mewar, the Rajputs met Babur at the Battle of Khanua, near Agra. But Babur was a brilliant leader, and he inspired his men to a great victory in the name of Islam.

By the time of his death in 1530, after a reign lasting only four years, Babur ruled an empire that stretched from Kabul across northern India to the borders of Bengal. He was buried in his favorite garden in Kabul.

HUMAYUN

A much weaker ruler than his father. Humayun (right) came under threat from his brothers and from the Afghans. His greatest achievement was often said to be his son, Akbar (left).

Legend says that Babur's last words to his son and heir, Humayun, were a warning not to do anything to harm his brothers – even though they might deserve it. His words were prophetic. Though trained for war from an early age, Humayun was a far weaker ruler than his father and had great difficulty keeping control over Babur's conquests in India. His four brothers, Mirza Sulaiman, Kamran, Askari, and Hindal were each given a province to govern. They were constantly in conflict with Humayun. Yet he treated them, as his father had advised, more leniently than they deserved. There was, however, an even greater threat to his throne.

WAR WITH SHER KHAN

The Afghan forces in the east continued to oppose the Mughals and still hoped to restore the Lodi dynasty, defeated by Babur at the Battle of Panipat. Their leader was an extremely able Afghan nobleman, called Sher Khan Sur. Humayun was slow to react to the growing threat posed by the Afghans. In 1537, Sher Khan invaded Bengal and defeated its ruler, Mahmud Shah. Humayun reached Bengal too late and was unable to save the kingdom. Months of bargaining over territory followed.

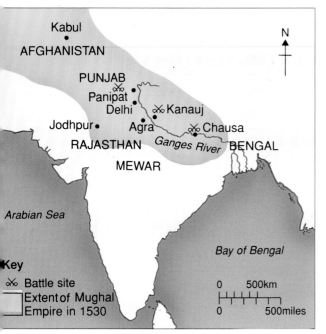

This map shows the extent of the Mughal Empire at the beginning of Humayun's reign in 1530, and the sites of the most important battles fought by Humayun and his father, Babur.

In 1539, the two armies clashed again at the Battle of Chausa on the banks of the Ganges River, where, in a surprise attack, the Mughals were almost completely annihilated by the Afghan forces. In the chaos that followed the battle, several members of Humayun's family were lost or taken prisoner by Sher Khan. Humayun himself had a narrow escape. The emperor's water-carrier filled a waterskin with air for Humayun to use as a float to cross the river.

In a ceremony after the battle, Sher Khan was crowned King of Hindustan and assumed the title Sher Shah. Humayun, meanwhile, fled to Agra for consultations with his brothers. Even at this critical time they could not agree what to do. The following year, Humayun faced Sher Shah's army once more at the Battle of Kanauj and, once more, was soundly beaten. For the next 15 years, the Afghan Sur dynasty ruled in the Mughals' place.

HUMAYUN IN EXILE

Humayun spent these years in exile, desperately trying to find a way of recovering his throne. In 1544 he crossed into Persia and asked the Safavid ruler, Shah Tahmasp, to give him and his followers a safe refuge. The Shah agreed on one condition — that Humayun, a Sunni Muslim, should accept the Shia faith (see page 11). Reluctantly, Humayun did as he was told. After this, Shah Tahmasp became much friendlier toward Humayun and his attempt to regain power. With troops and funds provided by the Persians, Humayun led his forces against his brother, Kamran, who had control of Afghanistan. Humayun captured Kabul in 1553, and took Kamran prisoner. For Humayun, this was the first step on the road back to India.

RETURN TO INDIA

Sher Shah died in 1545, after just five years on the throne. He was a talented general and skilled organizer. During his short reign, he set in place a central system of government in India, while continuing to campaign and expand his empire. His successors, however, were not able to hold the empire together. In 1553, it was divided into four provinces, which considerably weakened it. A terrible famine added to the problems faced by the Surs. The stage was set for Humayun's return. In late 1554, Humayun led his armies from Kabul into northern India and took control of the Punjab. By mid-1555, he had entered Delhi. Slowly but surely, Mughal power was being restored.

Humayun was not destined to rule for long. One day he was coming down the stairs from his library when he heard the call to prayer ringing out from the mosque. He knelt down on a step to pray. As he got up, he slipped and fell. He died on January 24, 1556.

Humayun's tomb in Delhi. It was built in the mid-16th century by Humayun's wife, Haji Begum. She is buried by her husband's side. The tomb's design is said to have influenced the architects of the Taj Mahal.

AKBAR THE GREAT

Akbar is usually considered to be the greatest Mughal emperor of all. He was born on October 15, 1542, in the small desert town of Umarkot in Sind, northwest India, as his father, Humayun, fled toward Persia. While still a young baby, Akbar was taken hostage by one of Humayun's rivals, his brother, Askari. No harm came to him, and he was reunited with his parents in November 1545. From an early age,

A scene from the Akbar-nama, Akbar's memoirs. It shows a young Akbar being taught to shoot by his guardian, Bairam Khan.

Akbar was involved in his father's campaigns, proving to be as able and as courageous a soldier as his grandfather, Babur, had been. At age ten, Akbar stood beside his father in battle. Two years later he led the army's charge into battle.

When Humayun died in Delhi in 1556, Akbar was campaigning hundreds of miles away to the north in Punjab. A messenger was sent to inform him of his father's death and to bring him back to take control of the empire. On February 14, 1556, Akbar was crowned emperor. He was only 13 years old. Humayun's trusted general, Bairam Khan, was appointed regent and Akbar's guardian. The task before them was to reconquer the lands lost by Humayun, only a fraction of which had been recovered, and to reestablish firm control over the expanding empire.

THREATS TO THE THRONE

The first threat to Akbar's authority came from Hemu, a Hindu general who had become chief minister of the Afghan prince, Adil Shah, a descendant of the great Sher Shah. In October 1556, Hemu launched a surprise attack on the Mughal forces in Delhi. He entered the city and declared himself emperor.

Despite the fall of Delhi, Akbar and Bairam Khan decided to attack Hemu. On November 5, 1556, the Mughals fought Hemu's army at the second Battle of Panipat. Hemu's larger force fought bravely, and the battle seemed to be turning against the Mughals when a lucky accident saved them. A stray arrow hit Hemu in the eye as he rode on top of his magnificent war elephant, and he fell unconscious. When his soldiers saw this, they assumed Hemu was dead and turned tail and fled. In fact, Hemu died later, and his body was taken before Akbar and beheaded. His head was sent to Kabul, and his body to Delhi to be displayed on a post as a warning to others. Thousands of his supporters were slaughtered, and their heads made into a victory tower. Delhi was back in Mughal hands.

BAIRAM KHAN AND ADHAN KHAN

In 1560, at the age of 18, Akbar rebelled against Bairam Khan's authority and decided to take matters into his own hands. Akbar's mother, Hamida, and his foster-brother, Adhan Khan, were jealous of Bairam Khan's power and influence, so they helped to plot his downfall. Akbar dismissed Bairam Khan as chief minister and sent him on a long pilgrimage to Mecca in Arabia, the Muslims' holiest city. By chance, Bairam Khan was murdered on the way by an Afghan whose father Bairam had killed in battle.

With Bairam Khan dead, Adhan Khan, Akbar's ruthless and ambitious foster-brother, seized his chance. He was put in command of the Mughal army that invaded the kingdom of Malwa. But Akbar soon came to regret this appointment. Adhan Khan's cruelty toward his prisoners knew no bounds, and he refused to share the spoils of battle, even with the emperor. Matters reached crisis point in late 1561. Feeling slighted by the appointment of another noble as chief minister, Adhan Khan attacked and killed him. Akbar was furious. He ordered his men to throw Adhan Khan to his death from the palace walls. The emperor was now well and truly in charge.

SIEGE AND CONQUEST

The ruins of the great Rajput fort of Chitor, a stronghold of Rajput power. After a siege lasting for six months, the fort finally fell to Akbar's army. It was a massive blow to Rajput hopes of resisting Mughal rule.

With control of the empire firmly his own, Akbar could concentrate on expanding his territories. His first and most difficult campaigns were against the Rajputs of Rajasthan who, despite being divided among themselves, were as difficult to defeat as ever. Until the Rajputs could be subdued, they posed a constant threat to Mughal power in northern India. After a successful campaign in Jaipur, Akbar led his army to the great Rajput fortress of Chitor. This was the capital of the kingdom of Mewar, the most important of the Rajput states.

The ruler of Mewar, Rana Udai Singh, refused to give in to Mughal threats, so Akbar laid siege to the fort. The siege lasted for six months, until February 1568. Inside the fort, the Rajput troops tried bravely to resist, but they were no match for the Mughal cannon and guns. When their leaders died in the fighting, the Rajput warriors killed themselves and their families, as was their custom, so that they did not fall into Mughal hands. Thousands of others were killed by the Mughals, and the fort itself was left in ruins. The following year, in February 1569, Akbar attacked and captured another Rajput fortress at Ranthambor. With the fall of these two great forts, Akbar gained control over almost the whole of Rajasthan.

This illustration from the Akbar-nama shows Akbar's forces laying siege to Ranthambor Fort, another Rajput stronghold. Having captured both Chitor and Ranthambor, Akbar entered into a crucial alliance with the Rajputs.

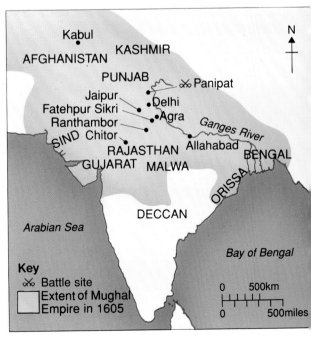

This map shows the extent of the Mughal Empire in 1605, at the end of Akbar's reign. By the time of his death, he had transformed the empire into the greatest power in India.

Many more triumphs followed. Akbar conquered Gujarat in 1573. He added Bengal to the empire in 1576. Kashmir followed in 1586, Orissa in 1592, and Sind in 1595. Between 1598 and 1601, he conquered a number of the Deccan kingdoms in the south. By the time of his death in October 1605, Mughal power stretched over half of India. To control the empire, Akbar set in place a central government that was linked to the provinces by a network of waterways and royal roads. This system remained in place for more than 200 years (see pages 42-45).

RELIGIOUS TOLERANCE

In 1562, Akbar married a Rajput princess, the daughter of the Hindu Raja of Amber. She became the mother of the future emperor, Jahangir. This was not simply a good marriage but also a political one because it helped to strengthen Akbar's ties with the powerful Rajputs and assure their cooperation. In return for favors shown to them, which included equal status with the Muslim nobles and some independence in their own kingdoms, the Rajput *rajas* (kings) remained loyal to Akbar. Their famous warriors fought in the Mughal army, and the *rajas* themselves served the empire as generals, governors, and administrators.

Marrying a Hindu was also a mark of Akbar's tolerance toward other religions. This, too, was based on sound political reasons. Akbar realized that if Mughal rule was to last in India, it must be accepted by both of the two main religions — Islam

A CLOSER LOOK

Although Akbar could not read or write, he had a great love of books and a magnificent library with some 24,000 manuscripts. (Recent research suggests that he may have had a reading disability.) His manuscripts were read to him by his courtiers. Like his father and grandfather, Akbar left a detailed chronicle of his life called the *Akbar-nama* which was compiled by his secretary, Abul Fazl. Every minute of court life was recorded, from affairs of state to what the emperor ate, drank, and said, births and marriages, the results of chess and card games, and any other "extraordinary phenomena."

and Hinduism. As part of this policy, he abolished the hated *jiziya* tax imposed on non-Muslims by the Delhi Sultanate, as well as the tax on Hindu pilgrims visiting their sacred sites. He also allowed Hindus who had been converted to Islam by force to return to their own religion without any penalty.

Akbar was deeply interested in different religions. At Fatehpur Sikri (see box), he built a large hall for religious debates. At first these debates were limited to Muslim theologians, but later Akbar invited Hindus, Jains, Parsis, and Jewish scholars to attend. In February 1580, three Jesuit fathers arrived at the Mughal court, at Akbar's invitation, to teach the

A CLOSER LOOK

In 1571, Akbar moved his capital from Agra to a newly built city about a day's march away to the west, called Fatehpur Sikri. Legend says that it was here that a Muslim holy man, Shaikh Salim Chisti, foretold the birth of Akbar's long-awaited son and heir, Salim (Jahangir). Filled with gratitude when the prophecy came true, Akbar built Fatehpur Sikri. In 1585, however, the city was abandoned, probably because of problems with the water supply. The city's exquisite red sandstone buildings still stand today.

The diwan-i-khas (hall of private audience) at Fatehpur Sikri. Akbar spent a great deal of time here, debating with religious scholars.

Among the Christians invited to Akbar's court at Fatehpur Sikri were three Jesuit priests from the Portuguese colony at Goa. In their accounts of their stay, they describe the emperor as wearing "a turban on his head, and the fabric of his costume was interwoven with gold thread.... On his brow he wore several rows of pearls or precious stones."

emperor about Christianity. Their own accounts tell not only of the warm welcome they received but also of their disappointment at not being able to persuade the emperor to become a Christian.

In 1582, Akbar announced that he was creating his own new religion called the *Din-i-Ilahi*, or Religion of God. In it, he sought to bring together all the best points from the religions he had studied. Not everyone approved. Akbar's liberal attitude toward other religions caused great resentment among the orthodox Muslim leaders, called the *ulema*, at his court. They feared that the emperor was rejecting Islam and undermining their own religious authority.

LAST YEARS AND LEGACY

The last years of Akbar's long reign were marked by the rebellious behavior of his eldest son, Salim, who later became Emperor Jahangir. In July 1600, while his father was campaigning in the Deccan, Salim tried unsuccessfully to seize power in Agra. In May 1602, from his base in Allahabad, Salim had the *khutba* read at Friday prayers and proclaimed himself emperor. Akbar recalled his trusted general and secretary, Abul Fazl, from the Deccan to deal with his troublesome son. But Salim had Abul Fazl assassinated, and he ordered the head sent to him in Allahabad. When news of the murder reached Akbar, he was stricken with grief. It was only after various ladies of the court acted as peacemakers that Akbar and Salim were eventually reconciled.

Akbar died on October 25, 1605. From his deathbed, he placed his own turban on Salim's head

One of the red sandstone gateways leading to Akbar's tomb at Sikandra, north of Agra. The building was begun by Akbar and completed by his son, Jahangir. The tomb has four gateways — one Muslim, one Hindu, one Christian, and one Akbar's own mixture — to reflect the emperor's tolerant religious views.

and gave him Humayun's sword, declaring Salim emperor. In a reign lasting 49 years, Akbar had transformed the Mughal Empire from a loose collection of territories into the greatest power in India and made his mark as one of the most brilliant rulers of all time. This is how his son, Salim, described him: "In his appearance, he was of medium height, with wheat-colored skin, and black eyes and eyebrows. His beauty was of form rather than of face, with a broad chest and long arms. On his left nostril was a fleshy mole, very becoming, of the size of a pea, which doctors said was an omen of great wealth and glory. His voice was extremely loud, and in conversation he was witty and animated. His whole air and appearance had little of the worldly being but exhibited rather divine majesty."

AGE OF EXPANSION

The last three of the Great Mughals — Jahangir, Shah Jahan, and Aurangzeb — consolidated and built on the mighty empire established by Akbar. Under Jahangir and Shah Jahan, the empire enjoyed its golden age, with political stablility, a booming economy, exquisite paintings, and beautiful buildings. Under Aurangzeb, the empire reached its greatest territorial size. But it also began to show unmistakable signs of decline.

JAHANGIR

A painting of a zebra by Mansur, one of Jahangir's favorite artists. The writing down the side is believed to be Jahangir's own handwriting.

Salim was proclaimed emperor in Agra Fort on October 24, 1605, and took the title Jahangir, or "world seizer." He was 36 years old. From his father, Jahangir inherited a stable central government, a policy of religious tolerance, and a strong alliance with the Rajput *rajas* (kings). He continued to expand the empire, with further conquests in Rajasthan and the Deccan. Jahangir was famous for his cruelty and temper, but he also inherited his father's love of art and culture, with a particular interest in wildlife and nature. Under his patronage, the Mughal school of painting, begun by Akbar, reached its heights (see pages 48-51).

The first part of Jahangir's reign was peaceful, except for the rebellion of his eldest son, Khusrau. On the pretense of visiting his grandfather's tomb,

Khusrau assembled an army and confronted his father's troops outside Lahore. The battle that followed was short and bloody. Khusrau was captured but continued to plot to kill his father. He was eventually blinded, a common punishment in Mughal times.

RISE OF NUR JAHAN

In May 1611, Jahangir married the beautiful widow of a Mughal officer killed on campaign in Bengal. She was given the title Nur Jahan, the "light of the world" and quickly became the favorite of Jahangir's 20 wives. Nur Jahan was not only beautiful, she was also intelligent and highly ambitious, taking an active interest in affairs of state. She and her father, Itimad-ud-Daulah, soon became the emperor's most influential advisors. Her father and her brother, Asaf Khan, were promoted, and Nur Jahan formed an alliance with Jahangir's second son and heir, Prince Khurram (later Shah Jahan). Although Khurram was nominated to take over the throne, nothing was certain in the Mughal court. Nur Jahan and her followers wanted to ensure that Khurram would become emperor after his father's death, with all the benefits of wealth and status that that would bring for them. In 1612, to strengthen their ties even further, Prince Khurram married Asaf Khan's daughter, Arjumand Banu, who later became famous as Mumtaz Mahal.

A CLOSER LOOK

Jahangir chose his favorite courtiers to become royal disciples. This was seen as a great honor. At a special ceremony, each disciple was given a tiny portrait of the emperor, set in gold and hanging from a gold chain. It later became fashionable for disciples to wear pearl earrings in each ear, as the emperor did.

AN EYEWITNESS ACCOUNT

Thomas Roe, England's first official ambassador to India, spent four years at Jahangir's court between 1615 and 1619. He had been sent by King James I to seek a trade treaty with the emperor. Roe was given a warm welcome and allowed to take part in the daily life of the court, even going with the emperor on military

Jahangir's son, Prince Khurram (later Shah Jahan) being weighed against bags of gold and silver on his birthday while his father (left) looks on. A similar ceremony was held on the emperor's birthday.

operations, or campaigns. Roe's account of his stay provides a fascinating look at Mughal life. He even describes the extraordinary ceremony that was held on the emperor's birthday. The emperor sat on a huge pair of golden scales and was weighed against gold and precious stones. Roe writes: "Suddenly the emperor entered the scales, and there was put in against him many bags to match his weight, which were changed six times, and they say were filled with silver... after with gold and jewels and precious stones (though it being in bags, might be pebbles); then against cloths of gold, silk, linen, spices, and all sorts of goods. Lastly came grain, butter, and corn."

Afterward, the goods were given to charity, and Jahangir scattered fruits made out of silver among his courtiers.

FIGHT FOR POWER

Thomas Roe was present at court when Prince Khurram returned from a successful campaign in the Deccan. Jahangir rewarded his favorite son with great wealth and goods, pouring a tray of gold coins and another of jewels over his head. From now on, he announced, Khurram would be known as Shah Jahan, the king of the world. Shah Jahan was a brilliant general and diplomat. He had already helped to subdue the great Rana of Mewar who continued to defy Mughal rule. But his position as Jahangir's heir began to look less secure when Nur Jahan shifted her support to his younger brother, Shariyar. To protect his claim, Shah Jahan rebelled but was forced to make peace with his father and to send his two young sons, Dara Shukoh and Aurangzeb, to court as hostages.

In 1627, while in Kashmir, Jahangir fell seriously ill. He died within days, on October 28, on his way back to Lahore. Neither Shariyar nor Shah Jahan were with him. A messenger was dispatched to bring Shah Jahan back from the Deccan, and he started north at once. On January 19, 1628, Shah Jahan became emperor. Two days later, on Shah Jahan's orders, Shariyar, two nephews, and two cousins were executed, removing any threat to his throne.

SHAH JAHAN

A month after his coronation Shah Jahan was reunited with his two sons, Dara and Aurangzeb. But he had little time to enjoy family life. He had established his capital at Agra, in the great fort built by Akbar, when news of rebellion reached him from the Deccan. Once again Shah Jahan shifted his court and set off with his armies on campaign. His wife, Mumtaz Mahal, went with him. The campaign was running well when tragedy struck. On June 7, 1631, Mumtaz died as she was giving birth to her fourteenth child. The emperor was heartbroken. Mumtaz had been his closest companion and

Shah Jahan and his wife, Mumtaz Mahal. The emperor was devastated by her sudden death.

Worshipers arriving for Friday prayers at the great eastern gateway of the Jami Masjid in Delhi. Begun by Shah Jahan in 1644, the mosque took 14 years to build. The eastern gateway was originally opened only for the emperor.

advisor, and he discussed all affairs of state with her. It is said that Shah Jahan spent two years in deep mourning. In 1632, the emperor began work on a fitting monument for his wife on the bank of the Yamuna River near Agra. It was called the Taj Mahal (see page 53).

After Mumtaz's death, Shah Jahan left more and more of the business of war to his sons, though he continued to direct the expansion of the empire himself. He dedicated much of his time to his great passion for architecture, commissioning the greatest buildings of the Mughal period. Besides building the Taj Mahal, he restored and rebuilt Akbar's forts at Agra and Lahore. In 1648, he transferred his capital from Agra to Delhi where he built a new city, called Shahjahanabad. Here he constructed the Red Fort, so-called because of its red sandstone walls, and the Jami Masjid, the largest mosque in India. (See pages 52-53 for more about Mughal architecture.)

Shah Jahan out riding with his favorite son, Dara Shikoh. Dara was later killed by his brother and rival, Aurangzeb.

WAR OF SUCCESSION

Meanwhile, the empire continued to expand. Under the command of Dara, Aurangzeb, and their younger brothers, Murad and Shuja, the Mughal armies pushed on south into the Deccan and secured their positions in the east and northwest. But there was bitter rivalry between Dara and Aurangzeb. Dara was Shah Jahan's heir and favorite son and stayed at court with his father. Meanwhile, Aurangzeb was sent on campaign after campaign on his father's behalf. Despite his skill and great success as a military commander, especially in the Deccan, he was often criticized by his father in favor of Dara.

In September 1657, Shah Jahan became ill, and the bitterness between the four brothers exploded into a bloody struggle for the throne. While Dara assumed power, Shuja and Murad both declared themselves emperor. In early February 1658, Aurangzeb began the march back to the north. He defeated Dara and sent his army fleeing to Lahore. Then he laid siege to

A CLOSER LOOK

The vast wealth of the Mughal emperors was famous far and wide. For public appearances, Shah Jahan sat on the fabulous "Peacock Throne." The throne took seven years to build. It was covered in hundreds of priceless emeralds, rubies, diamonds, and pearls. The canopy over the throne was supported by twelve emerald pillars. Above the canopy stood the famous peacock, with a tail of blue sapphires, a body of gold inlaid with precious stones, and a large ruby at its breast from which there hung a huge pear-shaped pearl.

Shah Jahan seated on the exquisite Peacock Throne.

For the last eight years of his life, Shah Jahan was kept a prisoner in Agra Fort. From his quarters, he could gaze across the river at the Taj Mahal, the tomb of his beloved wife. This is the view he saw.

his father inside Agra Fort, cutting off the water supply and seizing the royal arsenals and treasuries. Shah Jahan surrendered on June 8, 1658. He remained Aurangzeb's prisoner until his death in 1666.

AURANGZEB

On July 21, 1658, Aurangzeb proclaimed himself emperor and took the title Alamgir, or "conqueror of the world." Then he continued his pursuit of Dara. The two armies met in Rajasthan in March 1659 in a three-day battle that Aurangzeb won. Dara survived but fled. When Aurangzeb returned to Delhi, in June, he arranged a second, much grander coronation. The *khutba* was read in his name to acknowledge his supreme power and coins struck in his honor. Two months later, Dara was brought to Delhi as Aurangzeb's prisoner and paraded in disgrace through the streets. He and his family were sentenced to death. Aurangzeb's two remaining brothers, Murad and Shuja, were also hunted down and killed.

Niccolao Manucci, an Italian adventurer, served first in Dara's army as an artilleryman and later under Aurangzeb. This is how he described Aurangzeb: "He was very different from his brothers, being very secretive and serious and carrying out his affairs in a hidden way. He was melancholy in

Emperor Aurangzeb, surrounded by his courtiers. The emperor was a strict Muslim. His court historian wrote, "He keeps the fast on Fridays... and reads the Friday prayers with the common people. He fasts during the holy month of Ramadan and reads the Holy Koran." But his religious narrow-mindedness made him many enemies and marked the beginning of the end for the Mughal Empire.

temperament... anxious to be seen as a man of wisdom and a lover of truth...."

Aurangzeb was a deeply pious man, a strict Sunni Muslim who read and studied the *Koran* and held frequent discussions with the Islamic theologians at court. Under his leadership, the Mughal Empire reached its greatest extent. But Aurangzeb's reign also signaled the beginning of the end. In his desire to make India an Islamic country, governed by the *Shari'ah* (Muslim law), Aurangzeb undid much of the good work of his predecessors. He abandoned Akbar's policy of religious tolerance and reintroduced the hated taxes on non-Muslims. He promoted Muslims, rather than Hindus, to positions of power at court and ruthlessly destroyed all new Hindu temples. He ended Mughal patronage of art and architecture, abolished court music and festivals, and banned the drinking of wine. His narrow-mindedness led to a great deal of mistrust and suspicion, alienating the Rajputs, and leading to rebellions against his rule by, among others, the Sikhs of Punjab and the Marathas (see page 41). The empire was greatly weakened as a result.

THE DECCAN CAMPAIGN

Aurangzeb's long reign falls into two parts. At first, the emperor kept his capital at Shahjahanabad (Delhi) in the north. Then, in 1681, determined to overthrow the remaining independent kingdoms of the south, he moved his court and the bulk of his army to the Deccan. He spent the rest of his life living in military camps. Aurangzeb succeeded in annexing the once great Deccan kingdoms of Golconda and Bijapur, but he failed to put down the

This map shows the Mughal Empire at the time of Aurangzeb's death in 1707. Under Aurangzeb, the empire reached its greatest extent. But it was not to grow any farther.

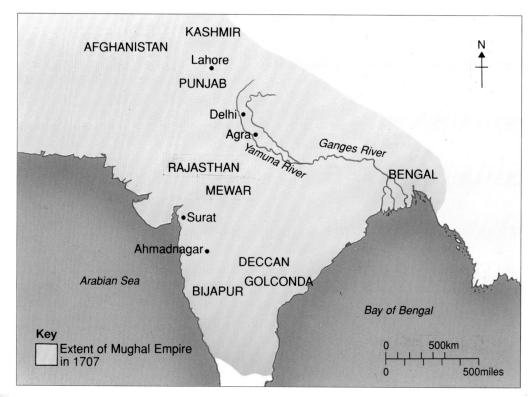

rebellious Marathas. As his Deccan campaign dragged on aimlessly, the emperor was losing control in the north. In his absence the administration grew lazy and corrupt. Local rulers began to reassert their authority. The endless wars drained the resources of the empire and emptied the imperial treasuries.

Aurangzeb died on March 3, 1707, in his camp at Ahmadnagar in the Deccan. The Mughal Empire was to last for another 150 years, but it was never the same force again.

SHIVAJI AND THE MARATHAS

The most serious threat to Aurangzeb's success in the south came from the Marathas, Hindus from the hills of the western Deccan. Their greatest leader — and Aurangzeb's archenemy — was Shivaji, a chieftain who rose from humble origins to become the symbol of Hindu resistance against the emperor's intolerance. Until his death in 1680, Shivaji constantly outwitted the Mughals, inflicting numerous defeats and carving out his own independent Maratha kingdom. Shivaji's adventures and exploits in battle became famous. In 1664 he raided Surat, the busiest port in western India, and seized the ships used by Muslim pilgrims on their way to Mecca, demanding a ransom for their release. Two years later, Shivaji was persuaded to visit the Mughal court in Agra. Snubbed by the emperor, Shivaji pretended to faint, was arrested and put into prison. But Shivaji tricked the guards and escaped, disguising himself as a Hindu holy man to avoid the Mughal patrols who were sent after him. Shivaji was succeeded by his son, Shambuji, whom Aurangzeb executed in 1689. Aurangzeb did not succeed in crushing Maratha opposition, however, and it revived strongly after his death.

A CLOSER LOOK

In the 17th century, the Sikh religion gained support in northern India. However, the Sikhs were persecuted under Aurangzeb, who ordered his officers to destroy Sikh *gurdwaras* as well as Hindu temples. In 1699 the tenth Guru, Gobind Singh, formed a band of Sikh warriors, called the *Khalsa*, to defend the Sikh faith. Members of the *Khalsa* had to wear five symbols to identify themselves as Sikhs. These were called the five Ks: *keshas* (uncut hair), *kangha* (a comb), *kirpan* (a sword), *kara* (a steel bracelet), and *kaccha* (a pair of shorts).

GOVERNMENT AND SOCIETY

At the time of the Mughals' arrival in India, much of the country was divided into independent states and kingdoms, each with its own chiefs and rulers. Under Akbar, a centralized system of government was set in place to make the empire easier to control and administer. So successful was this system that it remained in use from Akbar's time until the mid-19th century. At the very heart of the system was the emperor himself, the most important person in the Mughal Empire. He was the supreme head of state, commander-in-chief of the army, and the empire's chief judge. His word was law and could not be challenged.

ADMINISTRATION OF EMPIRE

The central government of the empire was divided into four main departments, each supervised by a minister. These were the *Diwan*, in charge of finances and taxes; the *Mir Bakshi*, in charge of military affairs and state intelligence; the *Mir Saman*, who ran the royal household and looked after the factories, stores, roads, and trade. The fourth minister was the *Qazi* or *Sadr*, who was in charge of legal and religious affairs. The emperor himself dealt with matters of diplomacy and foreign affairs. These ministers and their officers came from the ranks of the *mansabdars* (see page 43). Each had a huge staff of clerks, accountants, and messengers.

The empire itself was divided into different provinces, called *subahs*. Each was run along the same lines as the central government, with similar departments and ministers, who had to answer to their counterparts in the central government. The governor of each province was directly responsible to the emperor. News from the provinces was recorded by professional news-writers and carried by horseback back to court.

From an early age, Mughal noblemen were trained in the skills needed for war. These skills and their ability to muster troops for the army were vital for staying in favor with the emperor.

THE *MANSABDAR* SYSTEM

The main business of the Mughal Empire was war. Controlling the empire and conquering new territories took vast amounts of money and manpower. The army was, therefore, very important. Each officer of the state was given a rank, called a *mansab*, and was known as a *mansabdar*. In return, a *mansabdar* had to provide a certain number of troops for imperial service whenever they were needed. The *mansabdars* were divided into different grades, from a commander of 5,000 troops to a commander of 20. An ambitious young officer or nobleman could work his way up through the ranks. Grades between 7,000 to 10,000 troops were usually reserved only for members of the royal family.

The emperor appointed, promoted, and dismissed the *mansabdars* himself. Each received a salary, based on rank, from which he had to pay for the horses, elephants, carts, and equipment needed by his troops. In this way, the emperor could muster a huge, well-trained army largely at the *mansabdars'* expense. The *mansabdars* also acted as provincial governors or worked in other top administrative posts. Others were military commanders, recruiting and training the army.

43

The *mansabdars* were usually given new jobs and lands every few years so that they moved around the empire. This kept them from settling in one place for too long and building up local support, which might be used in rebellion against the emperor.

THE ARMY

The bulk of the Mughal army was made up of the cavalry troops provided by the *mansabdars*. There were also many thousands of infantry soldiers and newly introduced artillery (muskets and cannons), and a large troop of prized war elephants. In 1648, the army numbered about 200,000 cavalry, 40,000 infantry, and 500 elephants. Wherever it went, the army was accompanied by hundreds of elephants

War elephants played an important part in the Mughal army. Akbar grew so fond of his favorite war elephant that, when it died, he had a tomb built for it at Fatehpur Sikri. Here, Prince Murad, one of Shah Jahan's younger sons, fights for his life against his brother Aurangzeb at the Battle of Samugarh, in May 1658.

and camels, carrying equipment and supplies. There were portable workshops and offices, and even a traveling bazaar.

REVENUE COLLECTION

The vast royal treasuries of the Mughal emperors were filled with booty seized in battle, gifts from grateful subjects and visitors anxious to gain the emperor's favor, and taxes raised on agricultural produce and trade. Revenue from the land, which made up about two-thirds of state income, was collected in two ways. The empire was divided into crown lands and *jagirs*. On crown lands, taxes were collected by the emperor's agents and paid straight into the royal treasury. *Jagirs* were pieces of land transferred temporarily to the *mansabdars* who were responsible for collecting taxes. Part of this money went to make up the *mansabdars'* salary; the rest went into the treasury.

For poor farmers, this system could lead to great hardship. Up to half of their crops was taken in taxes, often with the use of force. François Bernier, a French doctor who spent 12 years at Aurangzeb's court, wrote that if poor people could not pay their taxes, any spare money and crops were confiscated and their children carried away and sold as slaves. Some people were forced to leave their villages and seek a living elsewhere.

TRADE AND INDUSTRY

During Mughal times trade flourished between India and Europe, Arabia, and Southeast Asia. Major exports included opium, spices, indigo, and textiles, such as silk and cotton, for which India was famous. Major imports included gold and silver bullion (bars) for making coins, horses for the Mughal cavalry, ivory, wine, and precious stones. There were two

A Mughal floor covering, from the reign of Shah Jahan.

major land routes toward the northwest, but these were very dangerous, so the bulk of trade went by river and sea. The major seaports were along the west coast, especially in Gujarat and Malabar. From Gujarat, merchants set sail for the Persian Gulf and Red Sea with cargoes of textiles and cotton cloth, dominating trade in the Indian Ocean region. The manufacture of cotton was the most important industry in Mughal India. The dyeing industry also flourished. Craftsmen made fine wooden goods, such as stools, chests, and boxes, leather goods, and embroidered shawls.

A CLOSER LOOK

At regular intervals along the royal highways were rest houses, called *sarais*. Here, traders and travelers could spend the night in relative safety, surrounded by high walls. The larger *sarais* had accommodation for 1,000 guests, their horses, carts, and camels. The gates were closed at dusk and opened at dawn.

A woman reeling cotton.

Wealthy Mughals loved beautiful jewelry, such as the exquisite pieces shown here. They are made of gold, set with rubies, diamonds, and other precious stones, and fringed with pearls.

Goods for the royal household were made in special workshops called *karkhanas*. These goods included guns and ammunition, carriages and litters, harnesses for the royal horses, tents, beds, turbans, and gold and silver jewelry. Only master craftsmen were employed in the *karkhanas*. If the emperor did them the honor of picking out a piece of their work for his own use, they were well rewarded for their skills. Any surplus goods were sold in the market.

LAW AND ORDER

There were several different systems of law and order in Mughal times. In the towns and cities, criminal cases were dealt with by judges, called *qazis*, in accordance with the *Shari'ah* (Islamic law), which based its rulings on the *Koran*. The emperor also held public audiences at court where people could present their grievances. In Shah Jahan's time, Wednesday was the day devoted to matters of justice. Sentences included fines, imprisonment, whipping, blinding, or execution. There were several different types of local courts. In Hindu villages, cases were brought before the *panchayat*, a council of village elders. Other courts dealt solely with financial matters, religious affairs, or general cases.

A CLOSER LOOK

While the Mughal emperors lived in luxury, the great majority of people worked as poor peasant farmers, growing crops such as rice, wheat, pulses (peas, beans, and lentils), sugarcane, and cotton. Their lives were very hard. Then, as now, they relied on the monsoon rains to water their crops. If the rains failed, or were too heavy, famine often followed. During the reign of Shah Jahan, a terrible famine struck Gujarat. It lasted from 1630 to 1632 and claimed some three million lives. One English traveler reported that people were so desperately hungry they even tried to eat each other.

ART AND CULTURE

Visitors to the Mughal imperial court were dazzled by its luxury and splendor. The emperors were immensely wealthy and surrounded themselves with the finest of everything. They were also very refined and became great patrons of the arts, leaving many great buildings and paintings as lasting memorials. At court, painters and musicians produced exquisite work at the emperor's command, in a style that mixed both Hindu and Islamic features. The Mughals were greatly influenced by Persian culture, which they considered to represent the height of beauty and sophistication. Mughal culture flourished under Akbar, Jahangir, and Shah Jahan, but it was discouraged under Aurangzeb.

LIFE AT COURT

Life at court was governed by strict rules of etiquette and elaborate court rituals. Each courtier knew his own place and the rights and privileges that went along with it. By standing in the wrong place or speaking out of turn, a courtier could cause great offense. Strict rules governed how a courtier might approach or speak to the emperor. If a courtier was in favor, he was allowed to stand closer to the throne. Less important courtiers stood farther away. Anyone granted an audience with the emperor had to bring a suitably sumptuous gift, ranging from gold coins to jewels,

A CLOSER LOOK

The ladies of the court were not allowed to be seen in public. They lived in separate quarters, called the harem, and watched events at court through screens. In Akbar's day, there were 5,000 women in the harem, including the emperor's 300 wives. Many were the daughters of local rulers anxious to win the emperor's favor. Besides being a hotbed for rumors and gossip, the harem was also a thriving business center. Nur Jahan, for example, made huge profits from trading in cloth and indigo.

slaves, and even elephants. As he approached the throne, he bowed, with the palm of his right hand pressed against his forehead. This showed his humility in the emperor's presence. Loyal service was rewarded with robes of honor, beautifully embroidered in gold and silver, and personally bestowed by the emperor.

The emperor's own daily routine was carefully planned and strictly followed. Thomas Roe described what happened at Jahangir's court. The court was awakened at dawn by musicians, and the emperor appeared on the palace balcony to show himself to

An illustration from the Akbar-nama *showing Akbar giving an audience. He is sitting on a raised balcony to show his high position. Beneath him are courtiers, officials, and visitors who have come to pay their respects. The most important are allowed to stand closest to the throne. On the table are gifts for the emperor.*

the people. This reassured them that he was alive and in good health, and that all was well in the empire. At midday, Jahangir appeared again on the balcony to watch an elephant fight or parade. In the afternoon, a great drum was sounded to announce the emperor's arrival in the *diwan-i-am*, the hall of public audience. Here appointments were made, injustices heard, and honors and promotions awarded by the emperor. He then met privately with his closest advisors to discuss affairs of state. This meeting often lasted late into the night.

MUGHAL PAINTING

The Mughal school of painting was created by Akbar. He set up an imperial studio at court, in which about a hundred artists, mostly Hindu, worked under the guidance of two Persian master

painters. They were given the task of producing exquisite miniature illustrations for Akbar's memoirs and of painting his portrait and those of his courtiers. From the study of unfinished paintings, historians have been able to discover how the Mughal artists worked. On paper that had been carefully polished, they made their preliminary drawings in red ink. After corrections, the sketches were redrawn in black. Then the paper was coated with a thin wash of white paint before the actual miniatures were painted in gouache. Details were added in gold leaf, and the whole painting was polished again.

The art of miniature painting reached its height under Akbar's son, Jahangir. He himself was a connoisseur, an expert, priding himself in recognizing the work of individual artists without being told their names. "As regards myself," Jahangir wrote in his memoirs, "my liking for painting and practice in judging it have reached such a point that when any work is brought before me, either of deceased artists or of the present-day, without being told their names, I say on the spur of the moment that it is the work of such and such a man. And if there is a picture containing many portraits, and each face is the work of a different master, I can say which face is the work of each."

Jahangir had a great love of nature and ordered his painters to record the plants, birds, and animals he saw. Artists were also on hand to record daily events and special ceremonies at court, and even went on hunting expeditions and into battle with the emperor.

FORMAL GARDENS

For the Mughal emperors, strolling in a peaceful garden was a welcome change from the work of running the empire.

The Mughal emperors loved gardens, where they could relax and shelter from the summer heat. Jahangir laid out several magnificent formal gardens in Lahore and Kashmir, his favorite place in India.

Water played an important part in Mughal garden design, cascading down terraces and gushing from fountains into pools. There were also shady marble pavilions, bridges, seats, and a huge variety of trees, flowers, and shrubs. On one visit to Kashmir, Jahangir and Nur Jahan put gold rings in the noses of the fish that swam in a garden pool. It is said that the fish in the pool today are descendants of those very same fish.

SPLENDID BUILDINGS

In addition to painting and garden design, the Mughals brought a new form of architecture to India, based on a mixture of Persian and Indian styles. The master builder of the Mughal emperors was Shah Jahan. Among his many achievements was the renovation and rebuilding of Agra Fort. In 1639, Shah Jahan began work on his new capital, the walled city of Shahjahanabad (the present city of Old Delhi). Here he built the magnificent Lal Qila (the Red Fort) on the west bank of the Yamuna River. The walls of the fort were made of red sandstone, over 98 feet (30 m) in height, while the buildings inside were of white marble, inlaid with gold and precious stones. The most exquisite was the *diwan-i-khas*, the hall of private audience, with its silver ceiling and the Peacock Throne as its magnificent centerpiece.

Not far from the Red Fort stood the Jami Masjid, the largest mosque in India, with space for 25,000 worshipers. Begun by Shah Jahan in 1644, and also built of red sandstone, the mosque had three grand gates. The eastern gate was reserved for the emperor's sole use. Both the Red Fort and Jami Masjid still stand today.

The towering sandstone walls of the Red Fort in Delhi, one of Shah Jahan's greatest works.

Shah Jahan's masterpiece, the Taj Mahal, is one of the world's greatest and most graceful buildings.

TAJ MAHAL

Shah Jahan's greatest masterpiece was the building of the breathtaking Taj Mahal in Agra as a tomb for his wife, Mumtaz. Construction began early in 1632 and took 22 years to complete. Some 22,000 people, recruited from all over India, worked on the Taj. Experts were brought from France and Italy to help with the decoration. The architect was Isa Khan from Shiraz, Persia.

Built of white marble, the Taj stands on a marble platform at the end of a formal garden. Beneath its dome lie the false tombs of Mumtaz Mahal and Shah Jahan, surrounded by a carved marble screen. The real tombs lie in an underground crypt. In an account of his travels in the Mughal Empire, François Bernier wrote, "I truly think that this great monument deserves much more to be counted among the wonders of the world than the pyramids of Egypt."

A CLOSER LOOK

Shah Jahan spent eight unhappy years in Agra Fort as Aurangzeb's prisoner (see page 38). From his quarters he could look across the river toward the Taj Mahal. A French jeweler, Jean-Baptiste Tavernier, who was traveling in India at the time, reported that Shah Jahan intended to build a black marble replica of the Taj on the opposite bank of the river. This would be his own tomb, linked to his wife's by a bridge. But Aurangzeb refused to carry out his plans and had his father buried next to Mumtaz. No one knows if the story of the black Taj is true.

53

The Empire in Decline

Although the empire lasted in name for another 150 years after Aurangzeb's death, his was the last great Mughal reign. Gradually, the central government was weakened by fighting and failing resources, and the emperor lost authority. The Maratha movement revived, and many independent kingdoms and states were created. With the emerging influence of the Europeans, first as traders, then as conquerors, the Mughal emperors became little more than puppets of the new rival powers. By 1756, the Mughal Empire was effectively over.

Aurangzeb's successors

In his will, Aurangzeb divided the empire between his three sons to prevent a bloody war of succession. But, after his death on March 3, 1707, the struggle for the throne began immediately. Prince Azam Shah proclaimed himself emperor and marched toward Agra. Meanwhile his elder brother, Shah Alam, had himself crowned emperor and took the title Bahadur Shah. The two met in battle in June 1707, outside Agra, with Bahadur Shah victorious. The third brother, Muhammad Kam Baksh, was killed in 1709. Bahadur Shah ruled for five years (1707-12). A much more moderate man than his father, he made a settlement with the Marathas, improved relations with the Rajputs, and took the last Sikh Guru into his service.

After Bahadur Shah's death in 1712, a new war of succession broke out, and chaos and disorder followed. Over the next few years, emperor followed emperor. In 1719, Muhammad Shah ascended the throne and ruled for the next 29 years. During his

Aurangzeb's eldest son, Shah Alam, became Emperor Bahadur Shah I in 1707. A capable ruler, he was already 64 years old when he came to the throne. His reign lasted only five years, and after his death, chaos broke out.

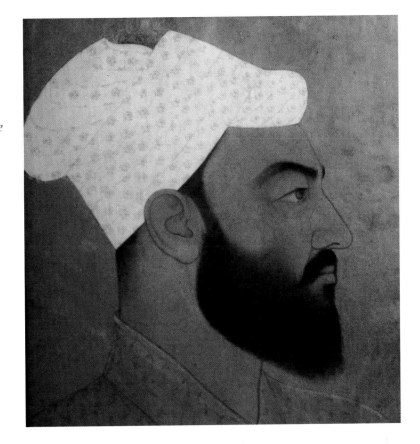

reign, the break up of the empire into a loosely-knit collection of regional states continued, and the emperor's authority declined even further.

DECLINE OF POWER

In 1739 the already tottering Mughal Empire suffered a disastrous blow. The Persian emperor, Nadir Shah, led his army into India. In February 1739 he met Muhammad Shah's army and easily defeated it. A month later he reached Delhi where he had the *khutba* read in his name. In the rioting that followed, more than 30,000 people were killed by the Persian troops. Muhammad Shah was forced to beg for mercy. The Persian emperor agreed to withdraw, but not before Muhammad Shah had handed over the keys to the royal treasury.

In 1756 Delhi found itself once more under attack, this time by the Afghan leader, Ahmad Shah, who had previously taken Punjab. In despair, the

Mughals called in their former enemies, the Marathas, to help them resist the Afghans. In the third Battle of Panipat, fought on January 7, 1761, the Marathas were badly beaten. Many thousands were massacred and thousands more taken prisoner. However, Ahmad Shah was never able to rule. His soldiers mutinied because of lack of pay, and he was forced to return to Afghanistan.

RISE OF THE EUROPEANS

Against this unstable background, the European powers in India were able to extend their influence and begin to fill the gap left by the decline of the Mughals. From the late 15th century, European merchants looked for new sailing routes to India and Southeast Asia, to take advantage of the flourishing trade in spices and other luxury goods. The first European to reach India by sea was the Portuguese navigator, Vasco da Gama, in 1498, looking, he said, for "Christians and spices." Further expeditions followed in 1500 and 1502. From their trading posts in Cochin and Goa on the west coast, the Portuguese crushed the opposition of the Mughal merchants and controlled the trade routes in the Indian Ocean for the next 100 years.

An illustration from the Akbar-nama *showing Portuguese merchants sailing the stormy seas to India. The Portuguese were the first Europeans to find a sea route to India.*

The Portuguese monopoly of Indian trade was broken early in the 17th century by Dutch and British traders. Each country set up its own rival East India company for the purpose of trading in India and Southeast Asia. While the Dutch traders concentrated their efforts on the spice trade in Southeast Asia, the British focused on India. In December 1612, the British set up their first trading post in India, at Surat on the west coast. By 1690 they had extended their influence all over India, establishing bases in Madras, Bombay, and Calcutta.

FROM TRADER TO CONQUEROR

The British established the city of Calcutta in Bengal in 1690 as a trading station for the East India Company. A factory was set up to produce saltpeter (an ingredient of gunpowder) and silk. A fort was built to protect the factory, and the East India Company's own garrison set to guard it. The fort was named Fort William. The city expanded rapidly. At this time the Mughal Empire was still a strong force under Aurangzeb, so the British had to petition the emperor for trading privileges and take care not to challenge his authority. By 1756, however, Bengal had become a semi-independent kingdom with a new, young ruler, Siraj-ud-Daula. Fearing the British threat to his power, he marched to Calcutta at the head of a large army. The British garrison was soon overwhelmed.

A 19th-century design of the East India Company's fortified factory at Fort William (Calcutta).

The British lieutenant general, Robert Clive, was sent to Calcutta to recapture the city. In June 1757, Clive led his troops against Siraj's army at the Battle of Plassey. Siraj was soundly beaten, and he himself captured and killed. However, the battle was not fiercely fought. Clive had made an agreement with one of Siraj's top military commanders, Mir Jafar, that he would not lead the bulk of Siraj's forces into battle. In return, Clive would make Mir Jafar ruler of Bengal in Siraj's place. In effect, control of Bengal passed almost entirely into East India Company hands. In 1764, the Mughal emperor, Shah Alam, granted the British the right to collect taxes and manage the economy in Bengal. Their success in Bengal marked a turning-point in the role of the British in India. The Company was

Robert Clive and the Nawab (ruler) of Bengal in 1773. The conquest of Bengal marked the start of British interest in gaining political control over India.

no longer just interested in trade. It now looked to extend its political control over the rest of India. In 1803, Shah Alam was taken under British protection. Officially he still ruled the empire from Delhi, but he was kept prisoner in the Red Fort and was under strict British supervision and control. This arrangement lasted for the remainder of the Mughal period.

FIRST INDIAN WAR OF INDEPENDENCE

As the power of the East India Company continued to expand, resentment grew among the Indians. On May 10, 1857, matters came to a head, sparked by a rumor. The majority of the troops employed by the British were Indian soldiers, called sepoys. They had been issued new rifles whose cartridges had to have the ends bitten off before the bullet inside could be fired. A rumor began that the cartridges had been greased with fat from cows (unacceptable to Hindus who consider cows sacred) and from pigs (unacceptable to Muslims who consider pigs unclean). The sepoys refused to use the cartridges and mutinied against their British officers. From Meerut near Delhi, where the mutiny began, events moved quickly. Adopting Bahadur Shah II as their figurehead, thousands of sepoys marched on Delhi, from where the rebellion spread through much of north India. At first, the British were slow to react, and for a while it looked as if the rebellion might succeed. But the rebellion had no real leaders or tactics, and soon

A CLOSER LOOK

The story of the famous Black Hole of Calcutta affected the way later generations in Britain regarded the Indians. It was reported that Siraj's men locked 145 prisoners up for the night in a tiny cell in Fort William. It was June, the hottest time of the year. Only 23 people survived the night; the rest died of suffocation. But some modern historians have questioned the story, claiming that the facts were exaggerated to stir up anti-Indian feeling.

The Indian Mutiny signaled growing unrest among Indians with British rule in India. Beneath the rumors of the contaminated cartridges lay resentment of the high taxes imposed by the British, and of British insensitivity about Indian customs and beliefs.

began to fizzle out. By June 1858, the chief rebel strongholds had fallen, and the British had regained control. The uprising became known to the British as the Indian Mutiny, and to Indians as the First War of Independence.

BRITISH RULE

Although the British regained control, the mutiny had been a shocking experience for them. The British government in London decided that the East India Company could no longer be trusted with running affairs in India. In 1858, the Company was abolished, and the government of India passed directly into the hands of the British government, acting on behalf of the Crown. A viceroy (governor) was appointed to rule. Bahadur Shah II, the last Mughal emperor, was charged with rebellion and sentenced to life imprisonment. He was exiled to Burma, where he died in 1862. In his place, Queen Victoria became Queen of India. In 1877 she was proclaimed Empress of India. A new age of empire had begun.

TIMELINE

711	Arabs conquer the western province of Sind.
1001	Mahmud of Ghazni, the Muslim ruler of Afghanistan, begins a series of raids into northwest India.
1025	Mahmud of Ghazni plunders Somnath temple.
1206	The Delhi Sultanate is founded by Qutb-ud-Din.
1236-40	Reign of Raziya Sultan, the first woman ruler in the Islamic world
1398	The Mongol leader, Timur, sacks the city of Delhi.
1498	Vasco da Gama of Portugal sails to India.
c. 1500	Founding of the Sikh religion by Guru Nanak
1526	Babur, the ruler of Kabul in Afghanistan, defeats the last sultan of Delhi at the Battle of Panipat. This marks the beginning of the Mughal Empire.
1526-30	Reign of Babur, the first great Mughal emperor
1530-40	First part of Humayun's reign
1540-55	The Afghan Sur dynasty defeat Humayun's army and rule India in the Mughals' place.
1555-56	Humayun regains his throne and restores Mughal rule.
1556-1605	Reign of Akbar the Great, who expands and consolidates the Mughal Empire. Akbar also sets in place a stable central government.
1556	At the second Battle of Panipat, Akbar defeats the Hindu general, Hemu.
1582	Akbar creates his own religion, the *Din-i-Ilahi*, or Religion of God.
1605-27	Reign of Jahangir, Akbar's son. Under his patronage, Mughal painting reaches its height.
1611	Jahangir marries Nur Jahan, the "light of the world."
1612	The British set up their first trading post at Surat.
1628-57	Reign of Shah Jahan
1630-32	Famine devastates Gujarat in western India.
1631	Death of Mumtaz Mahal, wife of Shah Jahan
1632	Shah Jahan begins building the Taj Mahal, as a memorial to Mumtaz. Construction takes 22 years.
1658-1707	Reign of Aurangzeb, the last Great Mughal
1680	Death of Shivaji, the Maratha chieftain
1707-12	Reign of Bahadur Shah I
1719-48	Reign of Muhammad Shah
1739	Delhi is sacked by Nadir Shah, king of Persia.
1757	At the Battle of Plassey, the British forces under Robert Clive defeat Siraj-ud-Daula, ruler of Bengal.
1761	At the third Battle of Panipat, the Marathas are defeated by the Afghan army of Ahmad Shah.
1857	Outbreak of the Indian Mutiny (the First War of Independence)
1858	Bahadur Shah II, the last Mughal emperor, is exiled to Burma by the British. He dies in 1862. The British rule India until 1947.

GLOSSARY

ambassador – a person sent by one ruler or leader on a mission to another.

artilleryman – a soldier who operates guns and cannons in the army.

caliph – a successor to the prophet Muhammad in the leadership of the Islamic world.

castes – classes, or groups, of people in Hindu society. These were traditionally based on the jobs people did.

Deccan – the high plateau of land in south-central India.

diwan-i-am – the hall of public audience in a Mughal palace.

diwan-i-khas – the hall of private audience in a Mughal palace.

dynasty - a ruling family.

enlightenment – being able to see the true meaning of life; being awakened.

harem – the separate quarters for women in a Mughal palace.

indigo – a blue powder obtained from plants that is used as a dye for cloth.

jagirs – pieces of land, given temporarily to the *mansabdars* by the emperor, together with the right to collect taxes from them.

Jesuits – members of the Roman Catholic Society of Jesus, founded by St. Ignatius Loyola in the 16th century.

jiziya – a yearly tax imposed on non-Muslims by Muslim rulers.

karkhanas – royal workshops where goods for the royal household were made by master craftsmen.

Khalsa – the military brotherhood of Sikhs, set up by Guru Gobind Singh, to fight Mughal persecution.

khutba – prayers recognizing an emperor's right to rule that were read in the mosque on Friday, the communal day of prayer.

mansabdars – Mughal officers and nobles given a particular rank and title according to the number of troops they could muster for the imperial army.

Mongols – nomadic peoples who lived in the great grasslands of Central Asia.

monsoon – seasonal winds occurring in Asia. In summer, they blow from the southwest, bringing heavy rains. In winter, they blow from the northeast.

mosque – a Muslim place of worship.

patronage – support or encouragement given to artistic or musical activities.

persecution – being badly treated for believing in a particular cause or religion.

pilgrimage – a journey made to a holy place, as an act of religious devotion.

qazis - Muslim judges in charge of upholding the *Shari'ah*, or holy law of Islam.

regent – a person appointed to rule on another's behalf because the rightful ruler is either too young, too ill or is absent.

sarais – public roadside inns or rest houses run for the benefit of travelers in Mughal times.

sepoys – Indian soldiers serving in the British army in India.

Shari'ah – the sacred law of Islam, as laid down in the *Koran* and in the Sunnah, or deeds, of Muhammad.

sultan – a Muslim sovereign or ruler.

theologians - people who study and are knowledgeable about religion.

ulema – men who are learned in the *Shari'ah*. The ulema was a very strong influence on the Mughal court.

FURTHER READING

Child, John. *The Rise of Islam.* "Biographical History Series." P. Bedrick Books, 1995

Dolcini, Donatella and Montessoro, Franceso. *India in the Islamic Era and Southeast Asia.* "History of the World" series. Raintree Steck-Vaughn, 1997

Dunn, John. *The Spread of Islam.* "World History" series. Lucent Books, 1996

Ganeri, Anita. *Exploration into India.* "New Discovery Books" series. Silver Burdett Press, 1994

Nugent, Nicholas. *India.* "World in View" series. Raintree Steck-Vaughn, 1991

Penney, Sue. *Islam.* "Discovering Religions" series. Raintree Steck-Vaughn, 1997

———. *Sikhism.* "Discovering Religions" series. Raintree Steck-Vaughn, 1997

Prior, Katherine. *The Indian Subcontinent.* "Origins Series." Watts, 1997

Wilkinson, Philip, and Michael Pollard. *The Magical East.* "Mysterious Places" series. Chelsea House, 1994

INDEX

© Evans Brothers Limited 1998